Painting with Buddha

Unearthing Creativity Through Spirituality

Table of Contents

Chapter 1. Introduction

Immerse yourself in the vibrant canvas of creativity as we journey through the enticing realm of 'Painting with Buddha: Unearthing Creativity Through Spirituality'. This Special Report narrates an extraordinary fusion of spirituality and art, allowing the reader to take a thrilling leap into the world of meditative painting. This ground-breaking exploration highlights the transformative power of mindfulness and spirituality in enhancing one's artistic prowess, revealing itself as an uplifting chorus of colors, emotions, and the profound silence of the Buddha. You'll be captivated by soul-stirring anecdotes, insightful tutorials, and vivid illustrations that foster and spring forth an elevated artistic vision. If you've ever yearned for the enriching union of the canvas and the soul, this compelling account is an absolute must-have. Embark on this spiritual voyage, and you'll undoubtedly unearth a wellspring of creativity you never knew you possessed!

Chapter 2. Unveiling Buddha in the Brushstrokes

Art is not a mere display of skill and prowess, it's an unveiling of the creator's soul. As we journey through the labyrinth of spirituality, let's meet at the crossroads where Buddhism intertwines with art.

=== Laying a Foundation: Understanding Buddhist Ideals

Buddhism as a religion and philosophy reflects an all-encompassing approach towards life, encompassing principles that guide the journey from suffering towards enlightenment—Dukkha, Samudaya, Nirodha, and Magga. Scribbles on a canvas transition into more than an aesthetic masterpiece when these spiritual elements begin to shape the artist's perspective.

Buddhist teachings emphasize the impermanence of life (Anicca), the concept of suffering (Dukkha), and the eternal change, or rather, lack of self (Anatta). These principles provide poignant insights into the human condition, and when reflected onto the canvas, can reveal art that transcends cultures, time, and space.

The first strokes on a canvas are thus, not just driven by an artistic impulse but a capture of these profound Buddhist ideologies. The practice of mindful creation allows for the blossoming of understanding, deeply intertwined with the spiritual journey of the artist.

=== Brushstrokes of Mindfulness: The Intersection of Spirituality and Creativity

The magic ensues when we truly immerse ourselves in the activity, setting aside doubts, judgments, and preconceptions. The Buddhist practice of mindfulness transcends meditation and finds its place in the heart of artistic creation as well.

To be mindful is to be present, observing the dance of bristles on the canvas, the merging of hues, the birth of patterns, and the sweet rhythm of breath. Every stroke becomes a meditative practice, transforming the canvas into a mirror reflecting one's mind, body, and soul.

The process of painting can epitomize the Buddhist teaching of 'non-attachment'. The moment an artist lets go of the 'end-result', stepping away from a deterministic approach, the creation process becomes free-flowing. It evolves organically, the canvas capturing raw, unfiltered expressions.

=== The Silent Conversations: Communicating through Colors and Symbols

Buddhist artistic traditions are rich with symbols that serve to convey deeper spiritual meanings. Brushes sing tales of Bodhi trees, lotus flowers, Dharma wheels, conch shells, and countless other symbols that have profound spiritual significance.

Colors, too, resonate with a deeper significance in Buddhism. The purity of a monk's saffron robe, the tranquility of the blue lotus, the fiery impermanence depicted in the red flames - each color evokes emotions, sentiments, and spirituality, allowing for a multi-dimensional dialogue with the viewer.

The incorporation of such symbols and color semantics in art serves as a bridge, connecting the conscious mind to the spiritual dimension.

=== The Sound of Silence: The Role of Meditation in Artistic Awakening

Meditation forms the backbone of Buddhist practice, and it undeniably permeates the channel of imaginative ideation as well. Our inner stillness often births the liveliest imaginations. Meditation helps tap into this tranquility, which then breathes life into art.

One might initially find it challenging to depict the profound silence that springs from meditation. But with practice, the silence begins to resonate. It unravels itself on the canvas in the form of thoughts, feelings, or simply as a burst of colors depicting serenity.

=== Unraveling Self and the Ephemeral World through Art

Art not only presents an opportunity to plunge into our deepest selves but also to make sense of the world around us. An understanding of the Buddhist concepts of impermanence (Anicca), suffering (Dukkha), and the non-self (Anatta) can dramatically shape the dynamics of this exploration.

For instance, the notion of Anicca emphasizes the transient nature of existence. It calls attention to the cycle of birth, growth, decay, and death. It's a reminder of the ephemeral beauty captured by cherry blossoms in full bloom or the lingering sunset on the horizon, their transient beauty captured forever through art.

=== The Culmination: Unveiling Buddha in the Brushstrokes

Art created with a Buddha-centric ethos encapsulates more than the serenity mirrored in Buddha's expressions. It is a journey of self-realization, a labyrinth through which wander, tracing paths of personal thoughts, emotions, spirituality, and philosophy.

The Buddha unveiled through mindfully guided brushstrokes does not merely represent the enlightened one; it represents the artist's journey towards enlightenment. Art thus becomes the medium of an extraordinary mystical dialogue, a conversation that transcends the spectrum of spoken languages, touching chords on a spiritual realm.

And so, the process of painting becomes a form of meditative practice, where the subconscious unravels itself onto the canvas, smooth stroke by smooth stroke. The journey is enlivened by the ethereal confluence of spiritual wisdom and creativity, culminating in a vibrant tableau echoing the silent, profound teachings of

Buddha. Dive deep, immerse yourself, and uncover a facet of yourself you never knew existed. Just like a lotus blooms amidst the muddy waters, your creativity can blossom amidst the silence and strokes of mindful unearthing.

Seize the brush, dip it into your soul, lay bare on the canvas your journey, etch out your path to spiritual and artistic liberation, and let the world bear witness to the Buddha unveiled through your brushstrokes.

Chapter 3. History of Spirituality in Art: An Overview

The longstanding relationship between art and spirituality is as old as human civilization itself. From the earliest cavemen, who found spirituality in the forces of nature and depicted their reverence through cave paintings, to contemporary artists using advanced mediums to communicate their spiritual experiences, art has been an undeniable instrument for the expression of spirituality. The encounter of art and spirituality is multifaceted and manifested in numerous manners across different cultures and ages.

3.1. The Prehistoric Connection

Prehistoric humanities connected deeply with nature and saw the divine in every aspect of their environment. This was a time when spirituality and art were one unified form of expression. Cave paintings from across the globe depict this spiritual connection that early humans felt with the natural world. These works – rendered with simple materials like charcoal, ochre, and animal fats – signify their awe, fear, and admiration for the elements. The images of animals, human forms, and abstract signs on the caves of Altamira, Lascaux, and other sites serve as the earliest examples of this union of art and spirituality.

3.2. Spirituality in Ancient Civilizations

As societies evolved, so too did their means of artistic expression and spiritual understanding. The ancient Egyptians imbued their art with spirituality, creating complex hieroglyphs and stunning artifacts to honor their pharaohs, gods, and the afterlife.

In contrast, the sublime sculptures and architecture of ancient Greece mirrored their polytheistic view, celebrating multiple gods with distinct roles. Key elements of Greek art, such as symmetry, perspective, and the portrayal of physical perfection, aimed to reflect the divine ideas of balance and beauty.

Meanwhile, in India, spirituality formed the core of artistic creations during the Indus Valley civilization. Later, Buddhist, Jain, and Hindu arts flourished, each with distinctive features but all deeply rooted in spiritual practice.

3.3. Spirituality and Renaissance Art

The Italian Renaissance marked a profound period indicating the resurgence of interest in ancient culture and spirituality's role in cultivating artistic expressions. During this period, art was a medium to communicate religious stories, concepts, and messages to the masses.

Artists like Leonardo da Vinci, Michelangelo, and Raphael reinvented the norms of visual representation through frescos, paintings, and sculptures. Works such as The Last Supper, Pieta, and The School of Athens explored religious narratives and philosophical inquiries with depth and subtlety. This era saw a clear blending of art and spirituality with creative techniques aimed at eliciting deeply spiritual responses from their audience.

3.4. Eastern Philosophy and Art

In the East, the philosophies of Taoism and Zen influenced Chinese, Japanese, and Korean art. Practitioners of these philosophies used painting and calligraphy as forms of meditation. The creation of a work of art, for them, was a spiritual journey towards enlightenment. Their art, mostly rendered in minimalist styles with an emphasis on blank spaces, aimed at capturing the essence of the subject - an approach often described as "less is more."

3.5. Modern Interpretations of Spirituality in Art

The modern period saw a break from traditional norms and conventions. As artists began to explore their inner spiritual experiences, the role of art expanded beyond simply depicting religious iconography or narratives. Artists such as Wassily Kandinsky, Piet Mondrian, and Mark Rothko used abstract forms and colors to express transcendental sentiments and spiritual dimensions.

3.6. Spirituality in Contemporary Art

In today's pluralistic society, contemporary artists employ a wide variety of mediums to express their spiritual ideas, grappling with concepts of identity, existence, and unity within a larger cosmos. Yoko Ono's 'Wish Tree,' James Turrell's 'Perceptual Cells', and Anish Kapoor's 'At the Edge of the World' all reflect on big cosmological ideas, evoking spiritual emotions and thoughts.

The journey of art and spirituality paints a fascinating narrative, demonstrating how art fostered and objectified human spiritual experiences throughout ages and cultures. The perpetual flux of spirituality is reflected in the changing contours of art, creating a rich, dynamic mosaic that symbolizes our diverse methods of exploring and understanding the spiritual world.

In conclusion, the aesthetic finesse of art and the profound depth of spirituality have always nurtured each other, each serving as a mirror to the other's essence. As we delve deeper into the canvas of mindfulness, the connection between spirituality and art becomes even more prominent, revealing that every stroke of color can be a step towards unearthing our inner Buddha.

Chapter 4. Meditative Techniques for Artists: A Deep Dive

Art can often be an outward expression of an inward journey, the point where spirituality and creativity unlock a higher level of consciousness. This marriage of art and meditation may seem unconventional, yet it is a path where significant artistic potential lies concealed. Initiating one's voyage into meditative techniques will result in newfound insights, enhancing the depth of artistic expression.

4.1. Understanding Meditation for Artists

Meditation's core essence resonates with the intrinsic tranquillity, the profound silence that empowers an artist to capture the intangible through visible strokes. It is a journey of becoming still to apprehend the subtleties of existence that often remain unnoticed. When an artist partakes in this voyage, it results in the resonant translation of this comprehension onto the canvas.

Delving into meditation doesn't involve dissociation from the external world; it's an intimate dance with reality, where an artist immerses themselves into the depth of experiences. One learns to witness the ephemeral nuances of nature, the stirring emotions within, to represent them through art passionately. The techniques we will explore seek to unearth this hidden potential in an artist to illuminate their work with the enlightenment of meditation.

4.2. Engaging the Senses

This first technique invites you to sharpen your senses. It starts with observing your surroundings and absorbing sensations with a renewed clarity. In the subsequent steps, you engage your senses singularly and together for a heightened perception of the world.

1. Begin by observing your surroundings intently, engaging your sight. Look at the objects, people, colors, lights, shadows around you with undivided attention.

2. Next, close your eyes and engage your hearing. Listen to the sounds in your surroundings: the chirping of birds, the rustling of leaves, or the bustling of city life.

3. Further, focus on touch. Feel the texture of the object closest to you. Try to comprehend the difference in surfaces; smooth, rough, or jagged.

4. Lastly, engage all your senses together. Open your eyes and try to perceive your surroundings employing all senses simultaneously.

When you tune your senses to work together, you perceive an image not just as a visual reformation but as an embodiment of various interconnected sensations.

4.3. Mindful Breathing

Breathing serves as the sustaining rhythm of life. By focusing on it, you can unearth a new understanding of your existence. It's a technique beneficial for calming the mind, and it reinforces a link with the present moment—the optimal state for artistic creation.

1. Sit comfortably in a quiet space. Close your eyes and turn your attention to your breathing.

2. Be mindful of the inhalation and exhalation. Do not control or alter the rhythm but become an observer.

3. If your mind begins to wander, gently bring it back to your breath.

4. Keep practicing this for a duration you're comfortable with and gradually increase the time as you progress.

4.4. The practice of Zazen

Zazen, or 'seated meditation', is a Zen Buddhist practice where one subtly shifts focus from the breath to the mind itself. This technique promotes self-observation and introspection.

1. Begin by sitting cross-legged, back straight, hands on your laps.

2. Close your eyes and follow your breath. Once calm, shift the focus inwards.

3. Do not suppress your thoughts or distract yourself; instead, allow thoughts to come and go, observing without judgment.

4. As insights surface, remember them for future application in your artistic creations.

4.5. Mindful Sketching

A meditative exercise explicitly designed for artists, mindful sketching can be a profound way to enhance observation skills.

1. Choose an object from your environment. Draw it without looking at your paper.

2. You should be absorbed with the object rather than the outcome of your sketch.

3. Identify the feelings of the object and let the emotions guide your hand.

Through these exercises, insights into your sensory perception and connections with the world can influence your artwork dramatically.

You'll be surprised at the depth of creativity that springs forth when your mind is still.

4.6. Walking Meditation

Art is often thought of as a stationary activity, linked to the confines of a studio. However, walking meditation—a practice that unifies movement and mindfulness—can stimulate your creativity in new ways.

1. Choose a quiet place for a walk, preferably enveloped by nature.

2. As you walk, keep your attention on the motion: the rhythm of your steps, how your feet feel as they touch the ground.

3. Let your senses engulf the environment— feel the breeze, listen to the birds, perceive the colors around you.

4. Walk with no destination in mind, focusing entirely on the journey.

As we traverse through the realm of art and meditation, the convergence of these complementary practices has the potential to lead you to a profound spiritual and artistic awakening. Experiment with these techniques, embrace their essence, and allow the fusion of spirituality and creativity to illuminate your artistic journey. Remember, it's not about the destination, but the vivid, mindful journey you undertake each time you pick up the brush. From an enriched connection with the present moment to self-discovery and transcendence, your art is set to embark on a unique journey towards artistic transcendence.

This sacred link brought forth by meditation invites you to deepen your relationship with art. Embark on this exhilarating voyage of self-awareness, and each canvas you touch with your renewed vision will radiate the enlightened symphony of your spirit. As Buddha rightfully exclaimed, "What you think, you become. What you feel, you attract. What you imagine, you create." So venture forth, harness your inflowing inspiration, and share your creative manifestation with the world in a waterfall of vibrant hues.

Chapter 5. Brushing with Awareness: Awakening to the Moment

The world whirls around us in constant and chaotic flux, yet at the fulcrum of this cacophony, there lies a singular moment, marked by profound tranquility and profound comprehension. This moment, bereft of distractions, brims with the clarity of existence, laden with the fullness of the now. As artists navigating the path of mindfulness, we are embarking on a journey to capture these fleeting moments of absolute presence and translate them into tangible art.

5.1. Becoming One with Your Tools

To paint with mindfulness means forming a deep, harmonious connection with your materials. Consider your paintbrush, the essential conduit linking your inner vision and the boundless canvas. It isn't just a tool, but rather an extension of your being, responding symbiotically to your every thought, every sensation, every rhythmic pulse of emotion coursing through your veins.

Spend meditative moments understanding the constitution of your brush. Where each strand joins, how the handle fits into your grip, the brush's weight—focus on these aspects meticulously. This connection will refine your brush movements, granting you more control and bringing soulful purpose to each stroke.

5.2. Observing the Color Spectrum

With each hue, there are a multitude of emotions awaiting our beckon. Take time to observe your color palette closely, understanding the unique energy each color possesses. Are the blues calm and soothing, or do they surge forth with kinetic energy? Are the reds seething with an intense vibrancy, or are they merely infusing a gentle warmth into your composition?

Create a chart with asciidoc markdown, listing each color and noting what emotion or sensation they evoke within you.

Color	Emotion or sensation
Blue	Peaceful, soothing, or energized
Red	Intense, vibrant, or warm

Intraindividual interpretations may vary. Record your personal experiences and emotions evoked by each colour. This record will later serve as a quick reference as you pour your emotions onto the canvas.

5.3. Listening to the Canvas Whisper

Every blank canvas holds myriad possibilities. It whispers to us, nudging us towards the creation that seeks to exist. As we tie the band of mindfulness around our artistic vision, we listen to the murmuring canvas, echoing its whispers through the gentle brush strokes.

Engage your senses, become intimately familiar with your canvas. Feel the texture under your fingertips, visually absorb its pristine whiteness, even inhale the altogether unique scent the blank page offers. This sensory acquaintance paves the way towards an empathic understanding, unlocking the silent dialogue between you and your canvas.

5.4. Painting: A Dance Unveiling the Present

In the grip of creative momentum, you may often find the surrounding world blurring into oblivion. Your focus sharpens to a fine point where nothing else matters save the incessant rhythm of the brush kissing the canvas. Introduce the calming cadence of mindful breathing when you paint, marrying your breath to each stroke.

Imagine it, the inhale as the brush dances back towards the palette, imbibing color, and the exhale as the brush glides across the canvas, its bristles unveiling a riot of emotions and thoughts. This mindful dance of creation is inseparable from the act of painting; it's how we forge deep, intimate connections with the world we put down on canvas.

5.5. Embracing Imperfection

One of the greatest insights that mindfulness brings along is the beauty of imperfection. As you paint, there will be strokes you deem less than perfect, perhaps even spoiling your envisioned masterpiece. But remember, in the realm of mindfulness, there are no missteps, only opportunities to grow.

This can be practiced while painting through accepting and surrendering to what exists on the canvas. Instead of viewing minor flaws with disdain, perceive them as integral parts of your creation. These unexpected twists impart an authentic uniqueness to your work, reflecting your journey toward mindful awakening.

5.6. A Deeper Perspective: The Shared Breath of Life

When we adopt the practice of mindful painting, we go beyond mere creation. Every stroke on the canvas breathes a life of its own, an echo of our existence. We connect with a deeper aspect of the Universe, a thread of universal consciousness. Every moment spent painting mindfully enhances our existence, binding us to the vibrancy of life and the stillness of the present moment.

Remember, painting is a sacred craft, merging the flow of creative energy from the Universe with our artistic vision. Beyond visual aesthetics, it's about creating something that lives and breathes, that speaks volumes about our existence.

As we lay down the palette and wash off the last flecks of paint, we realize this journey is far from over. The canvas might have been transformed, but so have we. By merging artistic expression with the tranquility of mindfulness, we have truly awakened to the moment, the fulcrum of our existence.

Chapter 6. Spiritual Landscapes: Interpreting Nature with Buddha

The world around us seethes with vivacity and wonder. The strands of this boundless beauty are interwoven in such multifarious arrangements that we often miss their significance. As an artist and spiritual aspirant, you must commune with these natural revelations, deciphering their profound tales onto your canvas.

To meditate upon and then emulate these captivating scenes on canvas is a transformative and empowering exercise. It requires a level of self-awareness and calm that can be achieved through the teachings of Buddha. As we go forth in this chapter, you shall learn how to pour your being onto the canvas, harmonizing with the serenity of nature under Buddha's guiding light.

6.1. Understanding Nature Through the Lens of Buddha

As you journey through the path of spiritual landscapes painting, the first step is observing the beauty of nature and interpreting its silent tales. This involves a mindful examination of the surroundings, an exercise well-envoked by Buddhist philosophies.

Buddha's teachings have always encouraged an attitude of being present in the moment, fully aware and perceptive of everything that surrounds you. This mindfulness is the essence of capturing landscapes in the vast canvases of our mind before transposing them onto a physical medium.

How do you observe a tree? Is it merely a tall structure with a spread of greenery or an intricate array of branches, each telling a different story? Is the sky merely a blue expanse, or a melody of colors in riveting dialogue with each other? Do the leaves scattered on the ground merely indicate the winding down of a season, or are they testament to the circle of life and death?

Submerge in the silence, and let your senses unmask the enigmatic essence of nature. Let your spirit resonate with this intimacy, landing you into a meditative state that swiftly finds union with your creativity and sprouts an unending fountain of inspiration.

6.2. Integrating Spiritual Mindfulness in Painting

Transmitting this profound observation onto your canvas is a dance between your inner universe and the outer manifestation of paints and brushes. Start with a blank canvas, symbolic of the infinite potential that rests within us. Understand that each stroke you draw, each hue you blend, birth a newer version of the reality you perceive.

The act of painting must be unified with your meditative state. A sharp focus on each breath you take, each movement of your hand, and each whisper of your brush against the canvas. This focus is an emblem of your consciousness, anchoring you amidst the storm of thoughts that may strive to distract you.

As you lean onto this mindfulness, you'll find your spontaneous reactions steering your creation. The painting begins to take shape not just as a mere reflection of what your eyes perceive, but as an eloquent expression of your soul. Missteps are not errors but revelations of a reality that needs your attention. The clouds may leak beyond the outlines, the river may take an unexpected turn, but this chaos, when met with acceptance, leads to a balance on your canvas showcasing the harmony of nature.

With each painting, you'll notice an evolution – not just on your canvas but within your being. The art and artist, in this intimate embrace, grow and flourish together, embodying the Buddha's wisdom: "What we think, we become."

6.3. Embracing the Change: Colors of the Sky

One of the most striking aspects of nature that resonates with Buddhist teachings is the transient allure of the sky. Its captivating hues during sunrise and sunset, its dramatic transformation during the passing of seasons – every change it undertakes embodies the impermanence that Buddha emphasized on.

When painting a sunrise or a sunset, strive to perceive the multitude of colors. Observe how they collide and yet exist in profound harmony. It's not just about playing with yellows, oranges, and pinks but understanding the subtlety – the soothing streaks of purple at the edge of the horizon, where the sky meets the earth, or the gentle blend of blue and red giving birth to a tantalizing pink.

Integration of this transience within your painting flows naturally when you let the brush dance to the rhythm of your observations. Do not be afraid of the changing maze of colors. Embrace these evanescent moments and paint them with the empathy of understanding impermanence, a core philosophy of Buddha's teachings.

6.4. Befriending Shadows and Light: The Dance of Duality

Just as in life, in the art of landscape painting, shadows and highlights are crucial components. They can instill a sense of depth, mood, and realism in your work. But more profound is their underlying symbolism under the illumination of Buddha's teachings on duality – the co-existence of light and darkness, akin to joy and suffering in our lives.

In the context of painting, the use of shadows brings forth the roundedness of the objects, giving them a tactile depth. The interplay of light and darkness is a delicate dance that turns a two-dimensional canvas into a three-dimensional window of reality.

While rendering your observations onto the canvas, be mindful of where the light hits and where the shadows loom. Shadows aren't merely the absence of light; they are narratives of objects interacting with light, with each other. Thus, do not paint shadows merely as darker regions. Observe their hues – the blueish tint in a shadow on a sunny day, the different shades cast by different objects, and the proportionality of the shadows giving a sense of distance and depth.

An enlightened artist, thus, accepts and understands the necessity of this duality, reflecting the simple truth that it isn't about the absence of light within darkness, but the harmonious interplay between the two. Both light and shadow, joy and suffering, are integral to the circle of life, integral to your painting, mirroring the wisdom of Buddha: "There is no path to happiness: happiness is the path."

As you further your excursion into the enchanting journey of painting spiritual landscapes, let your strokes imbibe and display the tranquility of nature, the reflections of Buddhist teachings. Merge with the rhythm of your breath, temper your strokes with mindfulness, and let your canvas become a meditative mirror to your soul. Always remember – with every stroke filled with genuine emotion and mindfulness, you are not just creating a painting, but you are becoming the very art itself.

Chapter 7. Coloring Emotions: A Journey Within

Oftentimes, it is said that every color speaks to the heart and caresses the soul in its unique way, voicing its distinct energy and emotion. In the intricate dance of light and color, our emotions find an expressive outlet. The process of uncovering them, translating them and manifesting them on canvas is an exhilarating journey, flavored with both poignant and pleasant moments.

7.1. The Emotional Spectrum of Colors

Colors hold an innate ability to invoke emotions. Each hue carries a certain vibe with its stroke - a vibe that can affect mood, trigger memories, and even evoke comprehensive landscapes of feelings. Our emotional response to colors can radically differ, being shaped by an array of factors such as culture, personal experiences, or even psychological and biological predispositions.

Let's delve into the emotional palette. Red, for instance, is usually associated with love, anger, excitement, and passion. The color Green resonates with tranquillity, freshness, and prosperity. Blue embodies peace, confidence, and calmness, whereas Yellow mirrors joy, energy, and warmth. These nascent vibrations are your initial guides as you begin etching emotions onto your canvas.

7.2. Invoking Emotions through Color Therapy

Color therapy, or chromotherapy, reaffirms the powerful emotional influence colors wield. Certain hues can energize, while others can soothe. Mirroring these nuances on the canvas can be highly therapeutic, making painting a medium of healing, self-expression, and profound exploration.

When you paint with your heart, every stroke becomes a palpable emotion. Transcribing this internal dynamic onto your canvas begins with acknowledging how certain colors resonate within you. Don't resist yourself. Flow freely with your color sentiments. Allow your brush to waltz effortlessly with your emotions, your colors becoming the rhythm of your heart's tranquillity or turmoil.

On this journey of creating a visual landscape of emotions, do not shy away from exploring the darker or "less pleasing" colors. The charcoal blacks, the greys, and the deep blues hold within them the possibility of touching upon the profound layers of emotions, unearthing the depth in our existence.

7.3. Dynamics of Observation and Intuition

Observation and intuition go hand in hand when it comes to embodying emotions in our artwork. While the observation allows us to understand the emotion behind each color, intuition guides us in choosing the right hues for our emotional expression. It's a silent dialogue between your observing eyes, intuiting heart, and articulating hands.

Exercise sensitivity towards the energy of colors, nourishing your intuition in the process. Paint in silence, and you will hear the whisper of colors. Paint in harmony, letting go of the judgmental mind and, you will feel the rhythm of colors. This raw connection with what colors stir within you ultimately guides you on how you wish to generate an emotional response in your viewer.

7.4. Brushstrokes of Compassion and Insight

Painting, inherently, is a meditative progression, calming the ripples of our mind and nurturing our spirit. While vivid colors can encapsulate joy, excitement, and hope, subtler hues can create a serene atmosphere, encapsulating the realm of mindfulness and inner peace.

Stroke by stroke, emotion by emotion, layer by layer, let your painting tell a tale of your intricacies. This courage to show the world what lies within you is a profound step towards self-discovery itself. The Buddha's teachings of compassion and mindfulness echo in these silent expressions of the soul.

It is helpful to remember that unraveling the emotional capabilities of art cannot be a boxed-in, quantified, or restricted experience. It is as fluid as the currents of emotions themselves. It's a personal journey that is dynamic, evolving, and deeply intimate. Embrace this journey and unapologetically be your true self on the canvas.

In conclusion, coloring emotions onto a canvas is more than just an artistic endeavor; it's a spiritual voyage into the self. Every touch of color carries an emotional note. As you blend and diffuse these emotional hues onto your canvas, you give form to your inner world, making the invisible visible. Embrace this dynamic rendezvous with vulnerability and courage, mindfulness and observation - you never know what unseen corners of yourself you will explore, or what unprecedented spectrums of your spirit you might unveil through your artistry.

Chapter 8. Canvas as the Mind: Exploring Thoughts and Ideas

The mind, in its purest form, is a rich repository of thoughts, feelings, ideas, and experiences. It's a complex yet subtle canvas—dynamic and multidimensional—where myriad colors of emotions, perceptions, and inspirations intermingle to create unique, vibrant patterns. A painter, thus, who seeks to explore this intricate tapestry can uncover an untapped reservoir of creativity waiting to be harnessed.

8.1. Deciphering The Inner Universe

We, as humans, perceive the world around us through our mental filters transformed into thoughts. This complex realm of thoughts and ideas is not unlike the wide expanse of a blank canvas—an enormity that can behold and depict anything imaginable. When infusing the canvas with thoughts and ideas, we're not merely creating art. We're extending the dimensions of the mind onto a physical plane, tapping into the boundless potential that lies within.

The process of translating internal realities into tangible art is a deeply introspective one. It demands deep spiritual observation and an honest conversation with one's self. This wisdom of self-knowledge, remarkably reflected in Buddha's teachings, adds an invaluable depth to artwork, enriching it with profound meaning. As you give yourself permission to dive deeply into your thoughts and ideas, your canvas begins bearing the witness to this introspection.

8.2. The Mind-Canvas Parallelism

Understanding the connection between the mind and the canvas requires considering the nature of both. The mind, like an untouched canvas, is a vast expanse filled with endless potential. Every stroke you paint represents an idea, a thought that percolates from within. The canvas, in essence, becomes your mind materialized.

This relationship is a symbiotic one, where the canvas acts as a conduit for exploring your inner self. On a deeper level, it's about exploring your spiritual consciousness—the domain of subtler emotions, intangible experiences, and infinite creativity. While we paint our emotions and experiences, the canvas becomes a silent spectator, a medium emboldening our expressions. It echoes our ideas, catching whispers of our thoughts, and embodies them in a spectrum of colors.

Deeper spiritual practices, as taught by Buddha, can assist in eliminating any mental obstructions. This mental clarity promotes an enhanced sensitivity towards the inner self, fortifying our connection with the canvas.

8.3. Translating Thoughts to Artwork

The beauty of art rests not only in physical shades and strokes but in what fuels them. It's about every energy, emotion, and thought channeled from the mind onto the canvas. The transformation of subconscious narratives into visible, tangible art is what makes art a deeply spiritual endeavor.

By honing our ability to silence the noise and listen to the whispers of our inner selves, we can discover ideas far more profound than we think possible, just waiting to be articulated on the canvas. It is this silent communication with our internal universe that forms the essence of painting.

Following are some basic exercises aimed at cultivating this unfettered communication with one's self.

1. **Mindful Observation:** At the beginning of your art session, sit quietly for few moments, focusing on your breath. Allow thoughts to flow freely, taking note of them without judgment.

2. **Art Meditation:** Dedicate time to meditate on a piece of your painting. Dive into the depths of each color, line, and texture. Explore how they resonate with your feelings.

3. **Expressive Canvasing:** Abandon all stifling art rules for a moment. Let intuition guide your hand. Ponder on an emotion or a thought and express it without the constraint of form.

8.4. The Therapeutic Convergence of Mind and Canvas

Art has proven therapeutic attributes. The practice of transforming thoughts and ideas into art on canvas can potentially lead to tremendous mental health benefits. The canvas, mimicking the mind, provides a safe space to confront, express, and process complex emotions.

While painting, worries and anxieties fade into the background as the mind immerses in a sea of colors and forms. The inherent mindfulness in painting helps maintain focus and cultivates resilience against stress. The soothing rhythm of the brush against the canvas invites personal insight, introspection, and a tranquility akin to meditation—providing the artist a greater sense of emotional well-being.

This spiritual practice of projecting the mind onto the canvas sees the artist gaining deeper awareness and acceptance of their thoughts, ideas, and feelings—seeing them as strokes of paint, composed and decomposed on an eternal canvas called mind.

8.5. A Palette of Endless Possibilities

Embracing the mind as a canvas brims with infinite possibilities. The mind, filled with thoughts and ideas, just like the differing shades on a color palette, paints a picture unique to every individual. As painters, the challenge lies not just in wielding our brushes but in exploring our minds as we traverse our path. Every artwork thus becomes a snapshot of the journey, an intimate exploration of self.

In conclusion, aligning artistic pursuits with Buddha's wisdom can be a boon to nurture creativity, bringing forth a synergy between art and spiritual consciousness. The journey of exploring the canvas of our minds, paralleling it with the physical canvas, not only unravels the bond between art and spirituality but also offers a profound understanding of the self—a window to our mystic inner universe. What better way to begin a painter's journey than by exploring the depth of your thoughts and ideas, and painting them into reality!

Chapter 9. Cultivating Creativity: The Role of Rituals

Through the annals of history, rituals have formed an indispensable part of the human experience, beguiling us with its mystique and allure. Artists, historically considered as high priests of the aesthetic realm, frequently attribute their artistic brilliance to the meticulous execution of rituals. Much like a conduit, these rituals channel artistic and creative energies into a comprehensible form, allowing creation to take shape in the actual world. And when twined with the spiritual perspectives fostered through Buddhism, rituals adopt a divine hue, transforming themselves to be the bridges that lead you towards unhindered creative expression.

=== Unraveling the Essence of Rituals

Ritualistic practice, in its core ethos, taps into the aspects of our cognition that are beyond the grasp of the overtly analytical mind, thereby rending it the power to cultivate creativity in novel ways. They help us establish a rapport with the unseen, the unperturbed stillness within us that resonates with abundant creative potential. Essentially, rituals implant a sense of order and rhythm into the chaotic ebbs and flows of the creative mind, thereby providing a stable platform from where artists can launch into the eclectic world of their imagination.

Rituals function as powerful tools to prime our brain for specific tasks or modes of thought, effectively allowing us to modulate our mental state and align it with our creative requirements. The precision and repetition of ritualistic actions induce a state of focused mindfulness, suspending the rush of the mundane world, and opening the gateway to mental realms marked by amplified creative activity.

=== Harboring Creativity: The Ritualistic Approach

Rituals could be as simple as brewing a cup of tea before starting on a painting or arranging the colors on your palette in a specific order. These steps help condition your mind to transition into a state that's receptive to creative impulses. They serve as balm to soothe anxieties, the small walls we erect that hinder free exploration of our creative landscapes. Like time-tested mantras, they reinforce our faith in our abilities and foster a sense of stability amidst the chaotic storms of creativity.

Some artists choose to dive deeper, incorporating elaborate rituals involving meditation and spiritual practices. They may begin with a period of silence to cleanse the mind's canvas before starting the process of creation or light incense to fill the workspace with a calming aura, thereby ensuring a peaceful creative journey.

=== Rituals and Buddhism: A Harmonious Symbiosis

In the Buddhist tradition, rituals assume profound implications, creating an inseparable amalgamation of the physical and metaphysical. Artistically speaking, they establish a bridge that allows one to flow seamlessly between focused attention and free exploration, both of which are essential for the expression of creativity.

Buddha, in his infinite wisdom, bequeathed practices such as meditation and mindfulness that serve as perfect tools to prime the mind for the creative process. These practices encourage a balance between the rational and intuitive aspects of the brain, fostering the right conditions for creativity to thrive. Spiritual rituals foster acceptance, compassion, and oneness with nature, all of which can imbue the art with depth and meaning.

By assimilating these spiritual rituals into your art practice, you can transform the act of painting from a task to a journey, a meditation, or even a prayer. This approach helps dissolve the barriers between the self and the art, thereby ushering in a state of flow, a zone where creativity arises spontaneously, unburdened, and undiluted.

Crafting Your Unique Rituals

Every artist is unique, bringing to the canvas their exclusive mental landscapes and emotional colors. Thus, rituals cannot be prescriptive but need to be discovered through personal introspection and experimentation. As you authentically engage with your spiritual practices, you'll intuitively identify the rituals that tune your mind to the frequency of creativity.

The objective is to create a ritual that resounds with you on a personal level, capturing your individual process of stepping into your creative zone. Be it a prayer, a mantra, the silence of meditation, or a deeply personal symbolic action, your ritual should serve as a channel enabling the voyage from the regular thinking mind to the imaginative, creative mind.

Rituals: The Bridge to Transcendental Creativity

Once you succeed in integrating ritualistic practices into your art process, you open a portal to transcendental creativity - a place where creation isn't just aesthetic expression but becomes an act of spiritual communion. Viewing art as a spiritual practice can amplify its impact, both on the creator and the viewer. These depths to your creative process translate into your artwork, making it a beacon that shines with your unique light.

In conclusion, by integrating rituals drawn from spiritual insights, you lay the groundwork for your creativity to grow and prosper. Embracing this notion gives birth to a virtuous cycle where creativity stirs the soul and the soul, in turn, magnifies the creativity, leading to the creation of art that reaches out and resonates with others on a visceral, spiritual level.

Chapter 10. Learning from the Masterpiece: Buddha's Lessons in Artistry

Each artist finds their muse in various phenomena: the rustling leaves of a tree, the resonating hums of a bustling city, or the tender whispers of a silent night. Yet, some see the divine not outside, but within themselves, and that's when tranquility paints a masterpiece adorned with enlightenment. Let us delve into this chapter, a profound pilgrimage through Buddha's teachings and their parallels with artistry.

10.1. The Canvas of Enlightenment

Buddha showed us that life is much like a canvas. The colors that adorn our canvas are the experiences – both good and bad – and the brush strokes symbolize the choices we make. But he also taught us the art of mindful choice - selecting shades of positivity, forgiveness, and love over bitterness, resentment, and hate. In doing so, we can create a masterpiece that is as resilient as the canvas of life.

Meditative painting takes its roots in this profound philosophy. It is, in essence, a practice where an artist employs mindfulness and inner peace as catalysts. Each brush stroke embeds a thought, a whisper of the heart, a pulse of life. By consciously choosing to paint this way, we transpose the intangible aura of spirituality onto a tangible medium.

10.2. Unfolding the Sutra of the Brush

Buddha's wisdom rolls out the sutra, each verse a font of inspiration, akin to the stroke of a brush. Unraveling the deep spiritual depths he gives artists a conduit for transcending ordinary vision. This tutelage can be encapsulated in three significant lessons:

1. Mindful Observation: Buddha's teachings encourage a deep sense of observation. In terms of art, this is the ability to perceive beyond the superficial.

2. Emptiness and Fullness: Awaken to the dual aspects of existence and reflect them in your artwork. Emptiness and fullness, shadow and light, creation and dissolution are all part of the unified whole.

3. Interconnectedness of All Things: As with a well-composed painting, life is an intricate mix of interdependencies.

10.3. Painting the Emptiness

One of the most profound aspects of Buddha's teachings is emptiness or 'Shunyata'. On the surface, a canvas might seem devoid of any creative force or life. Still, once ignited with the spark of inspiration, it begins to reverberate with boundless potential.

Emptiness, according to Buddha, is a state of mind rather than an absence of matter or substance. In painting terms, it could symbolize the unblemished canvas awaiting the artist's touch. The vast stretches of nothingness are fields of opportunities, pregnant with unmanifest potential. They are not vacuums but vibrant spaces full of inherent beauty waiting to take form.

10.4. Materializing Interconnectedness

The world we live in is composed of interconnected realities, each one acting upon and because of the other. This concept finds repeated emphasis in Buddha's teachings.

Each stroke is inseparable from the other; a rather subtle color might lose its significance in isolation but becomes indispensable when part of the bigger picture. Similarly, a painting is not made up of individual strokes but rather their combination and harmony.

10.5. Play of Shadows and Light

Buddha's wisdom meshes beautifully with the fundamental principle of art - understanding light and darkness. Shadows, in Buddhism, symbolize life's sufferings and tribulations, while light represents the path of enlightenment that leads us out of these shadows.

The interplay of light and shadows in a painting crafts depth and perspective. This dynamic simultaneously exists in life as well. By embracing the light and the shadows of our lives, we forge a path of continuous growth and mindfulness, much like an artist tirelessly creating his masterpiece.

10.6. Conclusion

Buddha's teachings don't advocate escapism from the world's realities but encourage harmony with them. Recognizing and accepting this balance is key, not just in life but also in art. Integrating Buddha's lessons can act as an axis around which your brush moves, translating these teachings into inspired art.

Ultimately, painting with Buddha is not only about creating art, it's a spiritual path towards self-realization. With every brush stroke, you are sketching not just on a physical medium, but also etching thoughts and principles into your mind, thus evolving your self with each creation.

In all honesty, the masterpiece you paint won't just hang in a gallery; it will be a living, breathing embodiment of your spiritual journey on the canvas of life.

Chapter 11. Ending at the Beginning: The Paradoxical Path of Creative Enlightenment

Creative heights are shrouded in a haze of fascinating paradoxes, each one inviting the artist to delve within themselves and transcend the boundaries of their concurrent vision. The journey, be it a painter cradling their brush between fingers numbed by creativity or a sculptor molding life from inanimate clay, appears to be linear. It starts from arguably an urge, a thought, a shower of ideas, and leads to the grand revelation – the masterpiece.

Yet, when observed from the bird's-eye view of consciousness, it's circular – starting and ending at the same point of enlightenment. This is where we venture, right into this blurring enigma, a journey that ends right at its commencement, the beautiful paradox hence resulting.

11.1. The Harmonic Symphony of Creation

From the cavemen scribbling the first hieroglyphs on wall to the renowned artists painting soul-stirring murals, the urge to create is embedded in the very fabric of our existence. It is the ubiquitous language conveying realms our words often fall short to define. Painters guide their brushes over canvas, sculptors chip away at stone, poets find rhyme in reason, each of them reflecting the dance of creation playing ceaselessly in their cores.

This dance may start with a stroke, a splash of colors, clashing and blending. But it doesn't end with the final stroke or the fully realized composition. It finds completion within the artist, as they evolve, molded by their own creation, nurtured by the self-introspection every art form warrants. Completed pieces of art, thus, are not just expressions on canvas, paper, or stone - they are completed cycles of creation radiating off the creator themselves.

11.2. The Paradoxical Cycle vs Linear Journey

Human perception is bound by the illusion of linear time. We perceive creation as a journey with a starting point and an end destination. But could it be that creativity is not a journey but a cycle?

As a dynamic process - creativity doesn't have a fixed, finite beginning or end. Inspiration does not spark only at the start of a blank canvas, nor does it cease once the painting is deemed complete. Rather, it dances through the temporal spectrum interweaving imagination with reality. The beginning fuels the process, and the process then recycles as the seed for fresh beginnings. Envision creativity thus as an ocean, its waves crashing ashore only to retreat back into the ocean itself, replenishing and regenerating endlessly.

This perception change does not invalidate the linear creative process, but rather provides a novel perspective. It complements the understanding of how each creative endeavor– our thoughts, emotions, and experiences– are part of a larger artistic tapestry we collectively craft and reshape.

11.3. Creative Enlightenment: Entering the Cycle

Buddhist philosophy imparts the wisdom that everything is cyclic. Birth leads to death, which then leads to rebirth in the great wheel of life. This can be contemplated within the ambit of creativity as well – the birth of an idea, the death of the initial concept as it morphs and evolves, and the rebirth of the refined idea leading to the final masterpiece – and so it spins on.

Mindfulness and meditation allow us to tap into the inherent cyclic flow of creativity. As we silence our rushing thoughts and simply exist – observing without judgment – we reach a state of creative enlightenment. We superimpose this enlightened state onto our canvas, and the cycle continues. We do not merely create; we become part of creation itself.

11.4. The Resonating Aftershocks: Art as a Mirror

The cyclical nature of all things implies that every end reverberates, triggering a new beginning. This is observable in artistic endeavours. The joy, satisfaction, or 'aha' moment that accompanies the completion of an artwork, isn't the end - it forms a ripple effect, a resonating aftershock that shapes our subsequent creative bouts. The soul-stirring reaction from an audience, the personal experience of the 'flow' state, or the lessons learned from self-reflection - all these lay the foundation for future works of art. The canvas is then a mirror, etching and reflecting experiences and lessons that continually feed into creative endeavours, enhancing the creator.

11.5. The Grand Paradox: Seeking and Being

The grand paradox lies in the interstice of seeking and being. We seek creativity and enlightenment, strive to cultivate it, and harness it. But in truth, we are what we seek. Every stroke of the brush is a manifestation of our inner creativity and enlightenment; every nuance of color reflects the spectrum of our experiences, serving to remind us that we are already the vivid painting awaiting to be acknowledged.

In our endeavour to attain this realization, there's much to learn from Buddha's journey. A prince who had it all, yet sought more, only to understand that he already was what he sought. Similarly, as artists, we seek to express, to feel, to communicate, only to realize we already embody the grand narrative of creation. This realization brings us back to where we started, ending at the beginning.

Buddha's teachings point us towards this profound truth: the act of creation embodies the creator, and the creator inherently embodies all creation. The journey is thus not one way, linear – it circles back, taking us to the source, to our selves. Our true Creative Enlightenment lies not just at the end of the creative journey but also the beginning, completing the circle in a resplendently paradoxical path towards the unearthing of creativity through spirituality.

www.ingramcontent.com/pod-product-compliance
Lightning Source LLC
Chambersburg PA
CBHW071047260726
48661CB00007B/3187